RIDDLES & TRICK QUESTIONS

FOR KIDS AND FAMILY!

Puzzleland

Table of Contents

PUZZLELAND

Introduction

Riddles & Trick Questions For Kids and Family! is a fun riddle book that contains 150 short riddles and tricky brain teasers of low to medium difficulty. It's perfect for families, parties or even youth group events!

These brain teasers will challenge the wits of children of different age groups and we promise that adults will enjoy them as much as their kids will!

A friendly warning for the parents to keep in mind; don't be surprised if your kids outsmart you!

With this book you will keep your kids and their friends busy and entertained for hours!

- All riddles can be solved with logical thinking.
- Appropriate for children of age 7+ and young teens.
- Ideal for family fun!
- Great for getting fun conversation started at the dinner table!
- Teach your kids lateral thinking and thinking "outside of the box"!
- 100% kid appropriate material.

About Puzzleland

We make innovative puzzle books.

Our mission is to create amazing reading experiences that elevate your mind to a higher level of thinking.

Visit us at *www.amazon.com/author/puzzleland*

Thank you for purchasing this book! Feel free to send us your feedback and ideas for improvement at puzzlelandbooks@gmail.com.

Order the Kindle Version

This book is also available in kindle version, at a lower price. You can order the kindle version of *Riddles & Trick Questions for Kids and Family!* on Amazon.

Let's get started!

Riddles 1-30

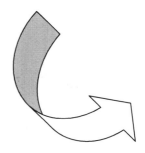

PUZZLELAND

1 Pencil on the Floor

How can you place a pencil on the floor of a room so that no one can jump over it?   [answer p.70]

2 The Yolk of the Egg

Which is correct to say, "The yolk of the egg is white" or "The yolk of the egg are white"?   [answer p.70]

3 The T Word

What starts with the letter "t", is filled with "t", and ends in "t"?   [answer p.70]

What Hour of the Day

What 4-letter hour of the day is spelled the same forwards and backwards? [answer p.70]

 The Longer Line

You draw a line on a paper. Using your pencil, but without touching that line again, can you make the line longer? [answer p.70]

 Ocean Without Water

Where can you find an ocean with no water and towns without people? [answer p.71]

7 Three Sticks

You have three sticks. Can you make four out of them without breaking any?   [answer p.71]

8 A Mistake

Can you find the the mistake?

1,2,3,4,5,6,7,8,9,10   [answer p.71]

9 The Farmer's Sheep

A farmer had 14 sheep, and all but 8 died. How many are left?   [answer p.71]

10 Throwing a Ball

How can you throw a ball 10 meters, and have it come back to you without hitting anything? [answer p.71]

11 Made of Glass

What has a body made of glass and a neck but no head?
[answer p.72]

12 Five Sons

Tom's mother has five sons named Eleven, Twelve, Thirteen, Fourteen... What is the name of the fifth son? [answer p.72]

13 Overtaking the Second Runner

You are participating in a race. If you overtake the second person, what position do you finish? [answer p.72]

14 In the Middle of March

What can be seen in the middle of March and April that cannot be seen at the beginning or end of either month? [answer p.72]

15 Word Starting With IS

What familiar word starts with IS, ends with AND, and has LA in the middle? [answer p.72]

16 I Have Four Legs

I have four legs but cannot walk. I hold food but I can't eat. What am I? [answer p.73]

17 Multiplying All the Numbers

What number do you get when you multiply all of the numbers on a telephone's number pad? [answer p.73]

18 Overtaking the Last Runner

You are participating in a race. You overtake the last runner. What position do you finish? [answer p.73]

Without Saying a Word

What language can you speak without saying a word out loud?   [answer p.73]

 **Three Stoves, One Match**

There are 3 stoves and you only have 1 match. The first stove is made of glass. The second stove is made of wood and the third stove is made of bricks. Which do you light up first?

[answer p.73]

21 How Many Birthdays

How many birthdays does a 50 year old man have?   [answer p.74]

22 Without a Head

What is higher without a head than with it and you can find it in your room?   [answer p.74]

23 4th of July

Do they have a 4th of July in Great Britain?   [answer p.74]

24 What Type of House

What type of house weighs the least?   [answer p.74]

25 Numbers with the Letter "A"

Name all the numbers from 1 - 100, which have the letter "a" in their spelling.   [answer p.74]

26 Through a Wall

What invention lets you look right through a wall?   [answer p.75]

27 A Letter You Can Drink

Which letter of the English alphabet can be drunk and served to guests?   [answer p.75]

 **Nine Pigs**

How do you fit nine pigs in eight boxes when each box only holds one?

[ ] [ ] [ ] [ ] [ ] [ ] [ ] [ ]   [answer p.75]

 **A Rooster on the Roof**

A rooster lays an egg on top of the barn roof. How can the rooster take the egg down on the grass without breaking it?
[answer p.75]

 **Without Getting Hurt**

What always falls without getting hurt and makes children happy?   [answer p.75]

Riddles 31-60

A Girl is Reading

A girl is sitting in her room at night. There are no lights on at all. There is no lamp, no candle, no light from any electronic device. Yet she is reading. How?   [answer p.76]

 **Building the Wall**

If it took four men 24 hours to build a wall, how long would it take two men to build the same wall?   [answer p.76]

 **The More it Dries**

What gets wetter and wetter the more it dries?   [answer p.76]

34 Less Sleep

During what month people sleep the least? [answer p.76]

35 From Chicago to California

A man is sitting in his cabin in Chicago. Three hours later he gets out of his cabin in California. How is this possible?

[answer p.76]

36 Twenty One Days Without Sleep

Can someone go twenty one days without getting sleep?

[answer p.77]

 **A Man With Beard**

A man shaves several times a day, yet he still has a beard. How is this possible? [answer p.77]

 **A Little Green Man**

What should you do when you see a little green man? [answer p.77]

 **A Room with No Walls**

What room has only a hat and no walls? [answer p.77]

 **How Much Dirt**

How much dirt is there in a hole 1 foot deep, 1 foot long and 1 foot wide?   [answer p.77]

 The Mysterious Third Man

One night, a king and a queen went into a castle. There was no one in this castle, and no one came into or out of the castle. In the morning, three people came out of the castle. Who were they?   [answer p.78]

 **Break it to Use it**

What is fragile but has to be broken before you can use it? [answer p.78]

 ## Two Mothers and Two Daughters

Two mothers and two daughters went out to eat. Everyone ate one sandwich, yet only three sandwiches were eaten in all. How is this possible? [answer p.78]

 ## After Sleep

What is the first thing you do after sleeping? [answer p.78]

 ## When No One Speaks

When no one speaks I am here. But the moment someone says a word, I am gone. What am I? [answer p.78]

46 I Bring you Light

I bring you light in the night. You love to burn me and watch me die. What am I?   [answer p.79]

You Will Cry

Take off my skin; I won't cry, but you will! What am I?

[answer p.79]

Taking Away 4 Oranges

If there are 6 oranges and you take away 4, how many do you have?   [answer p.79]

 **The Numbers on my Face**

If you look at the numbers on my face you won't find thirteen anyplace. What am I?   [answer p.79]

 **It Belongs to You**

What belongs to you but your mother and father use it more than you?   [answer p.79]

51 **Behind Each Other**

Jane and Jack want to sit behind each other in class and the teacher arranges them so they are both happy. How did she do so?   [answer p.80]

52 What Did you Eat?

You throw away the outside and cook the inside. Then you eat the outside and throw away the inside. What did you eat?

[answer p.80]

 What Clothes

What clothes does a house wear?   [answer p.80]

54 I Am the Second.

We are a family of 12 members. I am the second. I am also the youngest in our family. Who am I?   [answer p.80]

55 What Can You Catch?

What can you catch but not throw?   [answer p.80]

56 A List of Words

Which word does not belong in the following list:

flap clap snap trap wrap or slap?   [answer p.81]

57 Only One Letter

What begins with an "e", ends with an "e" and only has one letter in it?   [answer p.81]

 **Dropping an Egg**

A woman drops an egg onto the cement floor. The egg doesn't break after falling 2 feet. How is this possible?

[answer p.81]

 **One in Every Corner**

There is one in every corner and two in every room. What?

[answer p.81]

 **The Age of Marcus**

Marcus was 20 years old in 1780 but only 15 years old in 1785. How is this possible?   [answer p.81]

Riddles 61-90

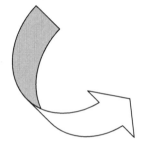

Ancient and New

What is as ancient as the earth but new every month?
[answer p.82]

 Everyone Has One

You have one. Madonna has one but she does not use it. Arnold Schwarzenegger has a big one and Johnny Depp's is quite small. What is it?   [answer p.82]

 **A Simple Addition**

What is half of 2+2?   [answer p.82]

 **Not a Hand**

What has a thumb and four fingers but is not – and never was – alive?   [answer p.82]

 **Round the House**

What goes round the house and in the house but never touches the house?   [answer p.82]

 **Bad Seven**

What did 7 eat?   [answer p.83]

 **I Carry Your Thoughts**

I can carry your thoughts. I can be dropped from the tallest building and survive,but drop me from the smallest ship into water and I won't.What am I?   [answer p.83]

 **Black, Red or White**

What is black when you get it, red and hot when you use it, and white when you are through with it?   [answer p.83]

 **Make One Disappear**

How do you make the number one disappear by adding one letter to it?   [answer p.83]

 **Mystery of the Night**

What is harder to catch the faster you run but never leaves you? [answer p.83]

Pronounced Wrong

I am always pronounced wrong, even by teachers and scholars. What am I? [answer p.84]

Miles Away

I don't have wings, but I can fly. I don't have eyes, but I can cry! I am miles away but you can see me. What am I? [answer p.84]

73 Daughters and Sons

Mom and Dad have two daughters, and each daughter has 1 brother. How many people are in the family?   [answer p.84]

The Chicken or the Eggs

What came first the chicken or the eggs?   [answer p.84]

75 How Many Houses

If you counted 12 houses on your right going to school and 12 houses on your left coming home, how many houses did you see?   [answer p.84]

76 Nine and Five

Which is correct, 9 and 5 is 13 or 9 plus 5 is 13?   [answer p.85]

77 You Can't Go In

What object has keys that open no locks and space that nothing fits in, and you can enter but not go in?   [answer p.85]

78 Twins, Triplets and Quadruplets

If you have two twins, three triplets and four quadruplets, how many people do you have?   [answer p.85]

 **Make 7 Even**

How can you make 7 even with one single operation? [answer p.85]

 **The Colored Houses**

Mr. Bluebird and his family live in a blue house. Mr. Greenbird and his family live in a green house. Who lives in the white house? [answer p.85]

 Dancing In the Sink

What is the job of the man dancing in the sink? [answer p.86]

Black and Blind

I am black and blind but can still see. When I sleep my head is down but over the ground. What am I?   [answer p.86]

 **On the Bus**

An empty bus pulls up to a stop and 8 people get on. At the next stop 4 people get off and 5 people get on. At the third stop 9 people get off. How many people are on the bus at this point?   [answer p.86]

 **Spelled Incorrectly**

Which word is spelled incorrectly in the dictionary?   [answer p.86]

 **Dying Eggs**

To dye a single Easter egg takes 8 minutes if you leave it in dye. How long would it take to dye 3 eggs?   [answer p.86]

 **Birds on the Tree**

There are 6 birds on a tree branch. A hunter shoots 1. How many birds are on the branch now?   [answer p.87]

 **Can't Escape Your Scold**

Every night you tell me what to do in the morning. Every morning I do what you told me. But I still don't escape your scold. What am I?   [answer p.87]

 **Three Pills**

You are sick and your doctor gives you 3 red pills. He tells you that you have to take one pill every half hour. How many hours later will you run out of pills?   [answer p.87]

 **Only in the Night**

What happens only in the middle of each month, in all of the seasons except summer and only in the night – never in the day?   [answer p.87]

 **Like a Parrot**

What's orange and sounds like a parrot?   [answer p.87]

44

Riddles 91-120

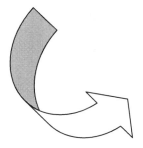

Two Squirrels Racing

Two squirrels are racing to the top of a coconut tree. The brown squirrel runs faster than the orange squirrel, but the orange squirrel is smarter than the brown squirrel. Who will eat the nuts first? The orange or the brown squirrel? [answer p.88]

 **Painting the Numbers**

James has been hired to paint the numbers 1 through 100 on 100 apartments. How many times with he have to paint 6? [answer p.88]

 **An Empty Basket**

How many apples can you put in an empty basket? [answer p.88]

 **Starts with Gas**

What has ten letters and starts with gas?   [answer p.88]

 **Sums Maniac**

How do you call a person who can't stop doing sums?

[answer p.88]

 **The Same Result**

What three numbers give the same result when added together and multiplied together?   [answer p.89]

97 Truck Driver

A truck driver goes down a one-way street the wrong way. A policeman sees him but doesn't arrest him. Why? [answer p.89]

 **Made Backwards**

What type of cheese is made backwards? [answer p.89]

 **In a Toaster**

What do you put in a toaster? [answer p.89]

100 How Many Books

There are some books on a bookshelf. If one book is the 3th from the left and 6th from the right, how many books are on the shelf? [answer p.89]

101 A Heavy Word

I am a heavy word, but backwords I am not. What am I?
[answer p.90]

102 Something Wrong

There is something wrong with one of the words below. Can you find which word?

First – Second – Third – Forth – Fifth – Sixth – Seventh – Eighth [answer p.90]

103 To the Movies

You want to go the movies with two friends. If you're paying, is it cheaper to take one friend to the movies twice, or two friends to the movies at the same time? [answer p.90]

104 Always Hungry

I can eat anything and I am always hungry. But if I drink water, then I am just over! What Am I? [answer p.90]

105 Two Missing Letters

Can you find the missing letters?

MT_TF_S [answer p.90]

106 You Bury Me Alive

You bury me when I'm alive, and dig me up when I die. What am I?   [answer p.91]

Serving

Where can you serve that's not in a restaurant but you have to wear a uniform?   [answer p.91]

Ten Oranges

How do you divide 10 oranges equally to 11 children? All children should get equal portions. How can you do that?

[answer p.91]

 **A Month With 28 days**

Which month has 28 days?   [answer p.91]

 **Ice Cube in the Water**

On the table there is a full glass of water with a single ice cube. When the ice has melted, what will happen to the level of the water in the glass? Will it remain unchanged? Will it increase? Or will it decrease?   [answer p.91]

111 **The Strongest Bird**

What bird can lift the most?   [answer p.92]

112 All His Fingers

How do you call a man who does not have all his fingers on one hand? [answer p.92]

113 Only Three Syllables

Which word contains 26 letters but only three syllables?

[answer p.92]

114 What Can You Make

What can you make that no one can see but everyone near you can hear? [answer p.92]

115 Made by Light

What is dark but made by light? [answer p.92]

116 Where In Your House

Where in your house can you see the following sequence of letters?

ASDFGH [answer p.93]

117 U-Shaped

When I am open I am U-shaped and wet but when I am closed I am V-shaped and dry. What am I? [answer p.93]

118 Pushed Out of An Airplane

A man was pushed out of an airplane. He had no parachute and no help from anyone. How was he able to survive?

[answer p.93]

119 Half Of It Is Zero

What number can you take half of and leave zero? [answer p.93]

120 How Old Am I?

When my mother was 28, I was 8. Now she is twice as old as I am. How old am I? [answer p.93]

Riddles 121-150

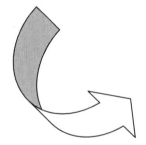

121 A Doctor and a Plumber

A doctor and a plumber are sitting in a room. One of them is the father of the other one's daughter. How is this possible?

[answer p.94]

122 On a Windy Day

I can only be played on a windy day. What am I?   [answer p.94]

123 Through Glass

I can go through glass without breaking it. What am I?

[answer p.94]

124 At 12 o'clock

At 12 o'clock, noon and midnight, the hour and minute hands of a clock are exactly coincident with each other. Between noon and midnight, how many other times do the hour and minute hands cross? [answer p.94]

125 How Many Fish

If you had twenty fish in your aquarium and 4 of them die right now, how many fish do you have? [answer p.94]

126 A Green Cave

There is a green cave. Inside the green cave there is a white cave. Inside the white cave there is a red lake. Inside the red lake there are a lot of black stones. What is it? [answer p.95]

127 Surrounded By Water

What state of the USA is surrounded by the most water?

[answer p.95]

128 Twenty One Eyes

I have six faces but no body. I have 21 eyes but I cannot see. What am I?   [answer p.95]

129 In the Rain

Jack, his mom and his dad went out in the rain. No one had a hat or an umbrella. But only two of them got their hair wet. Why?   [answer p.95]

130 Made of Water

I am made of water. But if you put me into water I will die. What am I?   [answer p.95]

131 How Many Chickens

There are 2 chickens in front of 2 other chickens. There are 2 chickens behind 2 other chickens. There are 2 chickens beside 2 other chickens. How many chickens are there?

[answer p.96]

132 Milking a Cow

What do you get if you milk a cow during an earthquake?

[answer p.96]

133 I Fix Your Mistakes

When you don't need me you ignore me. But every time you make a mistake you run to me for help and I fix your mistake. What am I?   [answer p.96]

The Last Three Letters

What are the last three letters in this order?

O, T, T, F, F, S, S, _, _ , _.   [answer p.96]

135 It's Midnight

It's midnight and it's raining. Will there be sunny weather in 48 hours?   [answer p.96]

136 A Letter With Water

Which letter of the alphabet contains the most water?
[answer p.97]

137 The Third Person

Two people left their house and went to the hospital. Three days later, three people left the hospital and returned to that house. Who is the third person? [answer p.97]

138 Make 5 Look Like 2

You have a piece of paper with the number 5 on it. Without writing anything, how can you make 5 look like 2? [answer p.97]

139 Always Ahead

What can't you see that is always ahead of you?   [answer p.97]

A Curious Letter

Which is the most curious letter of the alphabet?   [answer p.97]

141 In the Kitchen

Where in the kitchen can you find the following family of letters?   [answer p.98]

A,B,C, D,E, K

142 Find the Word

What does this mean?

Pot   oooooooo   [answer p.98]

143 Who Is This Man?

A man goes up 18 floors, he jumps out of a window and he survives. The next day, he goes up 20 floors, he jumps out of the window and again, he survives. Who is this man?
[answer p.98]

144 Never Inside Your House

I go around all the places, cities, towns and villages, but I never come inside any house. What am I?   [answer p.98]

145 Owls in the Dark

You are in the woods. It's dark and there are some owls around you. There are 22 eyes in the dark. How many owls are there? [answer p.98]

146 Without Touching It

It's yours but you can only hold it without seeing or touching it! What is that? [answer p.99]

147 Where in Your House

Where in your house can you see the following sequence of numbers?

28 29 30 31 1 [answer p.99]

148 Which Moves Faster?

Which moves faster than you? Heat or Cold?   [answer p.99]

149 Always Hot

It always stays hot even when you put it in the refrigerator! What is that?   [answer p.99]

150 How Many Contestants

In a race, the runner who came two places in front of the last man finished one ahead of the man who came sixth. How many contestants were there?   [answer p.99]

CONGRATULATIONS!

Congratulations on accepting the challenge and solving the riddles! We hope you enjoyed them!

Would you like to leave your feedback on this book? Your feedback will encourage us to create more quality books that suit your needs.

You can type the link below to easily leave your review in less than 1 minute:

34.gs/3fqw

Thank you for supporting our products!

Puzzleland

OTHER BOOKS BY PUZZLELAND

100 INTERACTIVE RIDDLES AND BRAIN TEASERS

The Best Short Riddles and Brain Teasers with Clues for Stretching and Entertaining your Mind

MEMORY IMPROVEMENT GAMES

A Complete Workout with 50+ Memory Exercises and Games to Improve Memory

TIC TAC TOE

8 Strategies to Win Every Game

WORD PICTURE SEARCH PUZZLES

Can You Find the Hidden Phrase, Object, Movie, Song or Place?

See all our products at www.amazon.com/author/puzzleland

ANSWERS

1. Answer:

You can put it next to the wall!

2.Answer:

Neither. Egg yolks are yellow.

3.Answer:

A teapot.

4.Answer:

Noon!

5.Answer:

You draw a shorter line next to it,
and your first line becomes the longer line.

6.Answer:

On a map!

7.Answer:

Make the figure "4" with the three sticks!

8.Answer:

Two "the" in the sentence
"Can you find the the mistake?"

9.Answer:

The 8 sheep that were left.

10.Answer:

Throw it straight up.

11.Answer:

A bottle.

12.Answer:

It's Tom, of course!

13.Answer:

If you take the second runner's place,
you arrive second.

14.Answer:

The letter "r".

15.Answer:

Island.

16. Answer:

A table.

17. Answer:

You get 0. Because if you multiply
any number with 0, you get 0.

18. Answer:

That question was a trap.
If you replied "second to last!",
you are wrong.
How can you overtake the last person?
It is not possible!

19. Answer:

Body language!

20. Answer:

You light the match first!

21. Answer:

Only one birthday –
the day he was born!

22. Answer:

A pillow!

23. Answer:

Yes they do, and a July 5th
and a July 6th. All countries
have a 4th of July, of course!

24. Answer:

A lighthouse!

25. Answer:

There is none!

26.Answer:

A window!

27.Answer:

T (Tea)!

28.Answer:

[N] [I] [N] [E] [P] [I] [G] [S]

29.Answer:

That was a trap question.
Roosters don't lay eggs.

30.Answer:

Snow.

31.Answer:

The girl is blind and is reading braille.

32.Answer:

To build the "same wall"?
No time at all!
The wall is already built.

33.Answer:

A towel.

34.Answer:

February (only 28 nights!)

35.Answer:

He is a pilot in
the cabin of an airplane.

36.Answer:

No problem.
He can sleep at night.

37.Answer:

He is a barber.

38.Answer:

Cross the road!

39.Answer:

A mushroom!

40.Answer:

None, or it wouldn't be a hole.

41.Answer:

The knight (night),
the king, and the queen!

42.Answer:

An egg.

43.Answer:

They were grandmother,
mother and daughter.

44.Answer:

Wake up!

45.Answer:

Silence.

46.Answer:

A candle.

47.Answer:

An onion.

48.Answer:

Four. The 4 you took!

49.Answer:

A clock.

50.Answer:

Your name.

51.Answer:

Jane and Jack are
sitting back to back.

52.Answer:

Corn.

53.Answer:

Address!

54.Answer:

February.
A year has 12 months.
February is the 2nd month.

55.Answer:

Cold.

56.Answer:

The word "or".

57.Answer:

An envelope!

58.Answer:

She drops it from higher
than 2 feet so after it falls 2 feet
it has not hit the floor
and broken yet.

59.Answer:

The letter "o".

60.Answer:

The dates are B.C.

61.Answer:

The moon.

62.Answer:

A surname.

63.Answer:

Half of 2 = 1.
So 1+2=3

64.Answer:

A glove.

65.Answer:

The sun.

66.Answer:

7 ate 9 (seven-eight-nine)!

67.Answer:

A piece of paper.

68.Answer:

Coal.

69.Answer:

Add the letter "G".
Then it's "Gone"!

70.Answer:

Your breath.

71.Answer:

The word "wrong".

72.Answer:

A cloud.

73.Answer:

5 (1 brother, 2 sisters and 2 parents)

74.Answer:

Eggs came first.
The argument is that long ago,
before there were chickens,
there were dinosaurs and
they laid eggs, too.

75.Answer:

12. They are the same houses.

76.Answer:

Neither. 9 and (or plus) 5
is 14, not 13.

77.Answer:

A keyboard.

78.Answer:

Nine people. Two twins are 2 people,
three triplets are 3 people,
and four quadruplets are 4 people.
 2 + 3 + 4 = 9.

79.Answer:

Remove the "s" from "seven"
and you get "even".

80.Answer:

The President and his family!

81.Answer:

Tap Dancer!

82.Answer:

A bat.

83.Answer:

Just one, the bus driver!

84.Answer:

Incorrectly!

85.Answer:

8 minutes.
Dye them all at once.

86.Answer:

None.All the other birds
got scared and flew away.

87.Answer:

An alarm clock.

88.Answer:

One hour later. You take 1 pill
right now (0 minutes),
1 pill after 30 minutes and
the 3rd pill after 60 minutes.

89.Answer:

The letter "n"!

90.Answer:

A carrot.

91.Answer:

None of them, because you
can't get nuts from a coconut tree!
Only coconuts!

92.Answer:

20 times.
(**6**, **16**, **26**, **36**, **46**, **56**, **60**, **61**, **62**, **63**,
64, **65**, **66**, **6**7, **68**, **69**, 76,86,96).

93.Answer:

Only one apple,
the basket will no longer
be empty after the first apple.

94.Answer:

An automobile!

95.Answer:

An addict!

96.Answer:

1,2 and 3.

97.Answer:

Because the truck driver was not in his truck. He was just walking down the street.

98.Answer:

EDAM cheese!

99.Answer:

You put bread, not toast!

100.Answer:

Eight books (you can sketch the problem out to solve it).

101. Answer:

The word "ton" (backwards it is "not").

102. Answer:

Forth. This should be Fourth.

103. Answer:

It's cheaper if you take two friends
at the same day (you buy three tickets).
If you go twice, you would have to buy
four tickets, two the first time and
two more the second time.

104. Answer:

Fire.

105. Answer:

W (Wednesday) and S (Saturday).
The letters are the days of the week.

106. Answer:

A plant.

107. Answer:

In the army.

108. Answer:

You juice the oranges and
serve 11 equal portions
of orange juice.

109. Answer:

All months have at least 28 days!

110. Answer:

The water level will remain
unchanged because the ice cube
displaces its own weight.

111. Answer:

A crane!

112. Answer:

Normal. It would not be normal
if he had all his (ten)
fingers on one hand!

113. Answer:

The Alphabet!

114. Answer:

Noise.

115. Answer:

Shadow.

116. Answer:

On a keyboard!

117. Answer:

An umbrella.

118. Answer:

The airplane was not flying.
It was on the runway.

119. Answer:

8. Take away the top half
and 0(zero) is left.

120. Answer:

The difference in age
is 20 years. So I must be
20 if my mother is twice as old.

121. Answer:

The plumber and the doctor
are husband and wife.

122. Answer:

A kite.

123. Answer:

Light (or sunrays).

124. Answer:

11 times.

125. Answer:

Technically you still have 20 fish
in your aquarium.
16 alive and 4 dead.

126. Answer:

A watermelon!

127. Answer:

Hawaii. All of it is surrounded
by water. Oddly enough,
most people would answer
Florida, California or Alaska.

128. Answer:

Dice.

129. Answer:

Jack's dad
was bald!

130. Answer:

Ice cubes.

131. Answer:

Just four chickens,
in a square formation.

132. Answer:

A milkshake!

133. Answer:

An eraser.

134. Answer:

...E,N,T
These are the first letters
of the numbers 1-10

135. Answer:

No, because in 48 hours
it will be midnight again.

136. Answer:

C (sea)!

137. Answer:

A baby! Those two people
were a couple, a man
and his expectant wife,
who gave birth to their baby.

138. Answer:

Turn the paper upside down
and look at it in a mirror.

139. Answer:

The Future (or, Tomorrow).

140. Answer:

Letter Y (Why)!

141. Answer:

These are vitamins! You can
find them in your refrigerator
(in food).

142. Answer:

Potatoes (Pot + eight o's)!

143. Answer:

A window washer!

144. Answer:

A street!

145. Answer:

10 owls. Not 11 owls,
because 2 of the eyes
are yours.

146. Answer:

Your breath.

147. Answer:

On a calendar. These
are days of a month.

148. Answer:

Heat. Because you can
catch cold but you
cannot catch heat.

149. Answer:

Hot peppers!

150. Answer:

There were 7 contestants.
The runner came in 5th place.

Recommended Books!